II

Love, Come Thou Near

Love, Come Thou Near

Robb Thomson

Love, Come Thou Near
Copyright ©2023 Robb Thomson

ISBN 9798218075118
Published by Robb Thomson LLC
250 Alameda Apt 3310
Santa Fe, NM 87501
robbm@cybermesa.com

Interior design by Robb Thomson
Cover design by Eric Thomson
Font: Bembo

All rights reserved. Copies and quotes from these poems can be made if proper citation is made to this book and its author.

Special thanks to my daughter, Judy Thomson for her encouragement and insightful line by line editing. The writing group at El Castillo have been helpful critics, especially its leader, Janie Chodosh.
Thanks are also due to my son, Eric Thomson, for his design of the cover.

Contents

Introit
Love, Come Thou Near   1

II Hegemon
Life in a World Hegemon   5

III

I	25
The Unfillled	26
A Valentine	27
Living Bonds	28
Gimme that Old Time Religion	30
A Shapeless Thing	32
Altruism	33
Ancient and Cranky	34
Family	35
Christmas	36
His Legacy	38
Mama	39
Me, Myself, and I	40
Love and Hate Together	41
My Uncle Gabe	42
Disarmed but not Disabled	44
Betting on Mankind	45
Humanity's Gamble	46
Drunken Words	49
The Next Comet	50
Love at First Sight	52
Nature Amused	55

On Being Great	56
On Love	57
Old Love	58
Patriot	60
Schubert Piano Sonata in B flat	61
Stuck in Purgatory	62
A Sunset	63
The Living Land	64
Last Laugh	65
When I Love my Friends	66
The Two Ways	67
Whose Country	68
Digital Futures	70
Challenge	71
Awe and Admiration	72
Why Not	74
Our Duty	76

I Introit

Love, Come Thou Near

Spirit locked in a body am I —
along with a whole slice of biology
naked to the space-time void
and glued to a speck of mud
endlessly tumbling in a vast maelstrom
of change.

Drunk with the heady potentiality of life,
we are propelled down the ages
on the sharp edge of a planet crammed with life,
to a milling society of self-aware humans,
bonded with an emergent interpersonal love,

a subjective bond
as strong as anything chemical,
and as time passes, capable
of continuing variation into new forms
and new ways of being experienced.

But change is accompanied with
all the clunky imperfections
we still embrace, like warfare
against other peoples and creatures,
together with utter exploitation of the planet,
both traits with the musty stink
of the grave about them.

Such is a dark side of evolution,
which also embraces
the stark probability of extinction,
proven over and again
on the real earth, from Greenland Norse
to Dodoes.

But Hear You ...
A prayer-song sounds
like an Easter hymn
over the funeral dirge:
"Here live loving humans,
who rebuff cold logic
with Love,"
in a cry that shakes
the foundations of
of Heaven and Hell.

Thus does the vast subjective world
brought to light by advancing life
become a sunrise
that banishes forever the night
of space-time
to a mystery future not to be foretold.

II Hegomon

Life in a World Hegemon

We are meaning-making animals. There is just enough mind in us to work with, and just enough animal left from Nature's ruthlessness to cancel all developing godliness. So we oscillate maddeningly from love and care for other living things to killing sprees and war, over a human time scale that can be discerned as distinct historical periods.

With nearly five-score years under my belt, I can easily discern five of the relevant modes of alarms and jolts of history that have brought us to our present condition.

1 The Roaring Twenties

Earliest Memory

Toddling up the walk
to my new home,
an urgency propelled me to
explore
the beckoning bricks
rising at the end of the walk,
where the mystery of my future
would unfold.

That was the house
my parents had just bought,

>   where I would spend the next 16 years
>   growing up.
>   It was at the bottom, but we called it home.

II The Depression

Though only 4 years old with two slightly younger
brothers
      when the Great Depression began,
      my memory is still full of images of that time,
      of gaunt men from hobotowns near the rail
      yards,
      walking the streets in ones and twos,
coupled with warnings from my folks
      to stay away from them —
      that they were dirty, and could be dangerous
      if we looked like we had money.

At the same time, stories in Sunday School told about
      how they were hungry and cold in the winter,
      and needed our help and sympathy.
There were stories about people who welcomed them
      to their back-kitchen doors with food
      in exchange for ouside help around the house.

But we kept our distance —
      when we asked where they came from,
      and why they didn't work like Dad
      and the neighbor men did,
      we were met with shrugs and evasion.

When the circus came to town,
> there was only one way to get inside the tent —
> load tomatoes from our backyard
> into our red wagon and peddle them
> to the neighbors.

So away we went up one street
> and down the next
> till the price of admission was in hand.

We must have been fun to watch,
> for as we went along, our school friends
> joined the joyful parade,
> and we became a kind of circus
> all our own.

It was not long till my younger brother, Junius,
> was trapped by a man with a car full
> of Saturday Evening Posts
> he was passing out to kids on the street
> to sell for him and his company,
> and he brought home strapped bags full
> of magazines for Dudley and me to sell
> to the neighbors.

I was now 7 and we were back on the street again,
> selling magazines for spending money.

Ensconced in our new project,
> our penny banks quickly filled,
> which led to a trip to the bank
> with Dad on a heady journey
> inside the grown-up world to start
> our own accounts with the surplus from

    our new business.

In the evenings Dad, in service of
    the family creed of self-sufficiency,
    drove us to distant
    neighborhoods to canvass
    for magazine sales.

We dared the dark porches
    and the intimidating
    full attention of quizzical adults
    as they opened their doors with
    our standard sales pitch,
"Do you want to buy a Saturday Evening Post?"
    followed by a quick retreat
    back down the porch stairs.

A kindly response of
    "How much is it?" was a big surprise,
    and we almost had to be dragged
    back from mid retreat for the sale.
When the adult's eyes glinted with annoyance,
    we were known to make
    the ultimate sales pitch,
"You don't want to buy a Saturday Evening Post, do
    you?"

The magazine period was followed by the newspaper period, setting the stage for all of us to later become first-generation college students.

We kids sensed the deep anxiety of our parents during this time when they set up an urban farm in our miniscule back yard with goats, chickens, rabbits and the occasional turkey. Our mother even peddled the excess milk to the neighbors.

We only learned of the crisis
      of Dad's near-firing well after the fact.
Though the Depression raged,
      we heard its thunder only distantly
      and our parents held our hands tightly
      as they guided us day by day
      through the storm.

Work on one hand
      and love and loyalty
      for family and community
      on the other
      is the human way,
and we learned it early and well.

III WW2

The Japanese attack on Pearl Harbor galvanized a country torn between America Firsters, who advocated staying far away from the European war, and those who realized we shared the danger from an expansionist Germany.

I felt the shock of the first news
      of the attack on the car radio
      as I drove home alone from church
      bathed in the comfort of
      normality — the familiar cadence
      of a Methodist sermon still in my ears,

        and the easy fellowship of my friends
        still embracing me.
My sense of security was momentarily untouched,
        and with my combativeness fully aroused,
        I was sure our navy would beat hell
        out of any one who dared to attack us
        on the seas.

The next day at school Assembly the bottom
        fell out of that confidence,
        as I and my fellow students
        heard the fateful words
"Yesterday, December 7…"
        from our president, and a stupefied nation
        found itself grievously hurt,
        and in a fight for its existence.

A high school senior,
        I was immediate cannon fodder,
        and with a new urgency,
        I rushed as fast as I could
        into the college major in physics
        I had dreamed about for years.
It was a war where technical proficiency
        was the key to winning,
        and everyone realized it from draft boards
        to military commanders.

So my draft board allowed me to remain
        in school for a couple of years,
        outside the orbit of the real war,
        till I was finally drafted

and exchanged civilian school
for the Naval version.

The brutality involved in the killing was implied
in the news more than described,
but anyone with any imagination
knew instinctively what the Philippine
death march and the bloodbath
at Guadalcanal meant to those actually there.
No one died an easy death in war.

Though my days were spent in school,
at nights I paid my dues to the times,
and the full savagery of war was acted out
in dreams of being gutted by a bayonet
or jumping ship into a watery grave.
Indeed, dreams were the vehicles that brought
war's full brutality home to me —
they goaded my days with a constant urgency
and I knew I was on borrowed time
from the horrors and danger of combat.

The biggest shock of the surprise attack was to find the Japanese had a better navy than we did, and only wonderful leadership, luck, and great bravery gave us the victory at Midway that turned the Pacific war in our favor.

Japan was starving at the end of the war, and militarily on its knees, but the Bushido spirit was so strong the military still wanted to fight even after the nuclear bombs had dropped.

Stopping the Pacific war even by the Emperor was a very near

thing.
So easy to start, war can be so hard to stop.

When the war ended, now an officer,
      my radar school was shut down
      and I was sent to Japan
      to be part of the occupying force.

I was stationed on the fleet flagship,
      a battleship anchored in Tokyo Bay
      opposite Yokohama, which had been
      a principle naval base.

From the ship, I could take a Navy launch
      to the landing pier
      and on my first trip,
      as I first stepped out of the launch
      the results of the fire bombing
      of Japan froze me in horror.

In front of me there was no city,
      only the scattered trash of one
      stretching as far as I could see.
An occasional concrete frame rose from the ground
      where an inhabited building used to be,
          thrusting from the ground like a broken finger.
Only the still existing checkerboard of roads laid claim
      to the fact I was looking at Yokohama.

But people still busily hurried here and there
      dressed in a kind of genderless garment
      that looked like a blanket wrapped

around their bodies and legs.
They lived in crude shacks slapped together
    out of the debris left from the bombing.

But in spite of its primitive starting point,
    life was beginning to reassert itself.

Tokyo was only a few miles away,
    and when I got there,
    its destruction was as complete
    as at Yokohama.
I headed for a well-known department store
    which of course had been bombed,
    but still operated at a much-reduced scale.
A couple of floors were still useable,
    but the main selling took place at tables
    on the sidewalk and in the street
    surrounding the store.
American service people like me
    composed a major part of the buying public,
    and as I wandered the store-on-street,
    a stack of woodblock prints
    caught my eye, and I bought a couple.
They were altogether out of place
    stacked on those tables,
    but I later learned the creator
    was a famous Japanese artist
    who had rejuvenated the ancient
    art of ukiyo-e — woodblock printing.
Walking away after the sale, I realized
    this great artist was selling
    his art treasures because he was hungry.

When we had leave from our duties,
        I would fill one of the fleet vehicles
        with men under me from my office
        and drive as far as we could in one day
        to see Japan on the fair-to-good roads
        that still existed.

On one of these excursions
        we came upon a city which had once
        held roughly 100,000 people.
On the road as we entered one side
        of the city, we could see the same road exiting
        the opposite side across a 10 mile stretch
        of shanties slung together
        by the remaining populace.

We stopped in the city center,
        as always, sobered by the awful destruction
        centered not on the military
        but on the people themselves,
        hoping to exchange a tentative word
        with an inhabitant.
But we were met with downcast eyes,
        and demurral.
We were taken aback by this diffidence
        not knowing what it meant,
        and with the exuberance of youth,
        not willing to accept complete
        separation for two peoples thrown together
        as we and they were by the end of the war.
Perhaps they remembered the "rape of Nanking"

>   by their own soldiers in their conquering
>   rampage through China,
>   and could not comprehend the American
>   way.

Normal give and take was maddeningly slow in coming.

IV Postwar Dominance

The war was a disaster to loser and victor alike — except for the US behind its precious oceans. We became a relative postwar colossus, our GDP, technology and science far above that of any other nation. Japan's science was smashed, and they turned to us to find new non-war connected fields to focus on.

A few years after the war's end,
>   I found myself a young faculty
>   member at the University of Illinois,
>   which was a leader in my branch of physics,
>   one of the fields the Japanese chose
>   to concentrate on.

They turned to us to teach them,
>   and became visiting faculty
>   and postdoctoral students
>   in my department.

I shared my office with the senior ones,
>   and although they were usually older than I,
>   we became permanent friends.

They never touched on their war experiences
>   and the hunger and homelessness

they must have known,
and I never mentioned my time in the Navy
and the total destruction I had witnessed.
I became the research advisor of one
of the younger postdoctoral students,
in a personal and research relationship that remained
for many years after he returned to Japan,
and a faculty position at one of their best universities
In this way I became close friends
with the future Japanese research leaders.

I visited Japan frequently
over my research career,
the highlight being a 6 month guest
with my family at a research center
in Tokyo now run by one of my friends.

One of our travels stands out in my memory.
It was to the university at Hiroshima,
which had been largely rebuilt after the Bomb.
My local host invited us to visit to the Bomb memorial, but I politely implied that my young children would not be part of the group.
My host turned to me
with an uncharacteristically direct expression
and insisted the children must go too,
implying that was the principal purpose of the invitation.

No Japanese ever speaks so emphatically — not ever,
    it being a major breach of etiquette,
    so I knew a great deal was suddenly at stake.
The children went to the Memorial,
    pawns in pain beyond their imagining
    as two guilty cultures grappled with their past.

With great effort and discipline, Japan put herself back together after the war, and it became a highly successful world competitor over the entire range of technology and manufacturing.

When I visited one of the successful carmakers
    early in their growth, there was no hint
    they would become so strong later.
I visited one of their major steel makers,
    and learned how they had taken the leadership
    in the field away from us by dogged attention
    and long term planning
    of the company's future.

It was heartening to see Japan rejuvenate itself
    not only physically, but also culturally.
The war convinced many Japanese
    that losing the war showed
    they lacked something the West had,
    and at first they shamelessly imitated us.

I witnessed the turnabout personally,
    when on one visit, I attended
    a recently constructed traditional theatre
    whose auditorium gave off
    a strong aroma of new wood

        to view a production of a Noh play —
one of the distinctive Japanese art forms
        developed for the old aristocracy.

Noh can be thought of as Greek tragedy
        translated into Japanese.
The slow movement and drawn out speech —
        which sounds like a western actor
        playing a soul raised from the dead —
        allows the listener to savor
        the stark tragic emotion being displayed,
        and in that way to deepen the tragedy
        of the drama.

The crowded audience was an enthusiastic group
        of mostly young people, and the actors
        were National Treasures who still
        mastered the highly rarified slow symbolic
        movements and speech of Noh.
The ambient emotion projected was very strong
        and the audience broke into clapping and cheers
        at crucial scenes in the production.

Sometime about 1975,
        I had a celebratory dinner
        with several of the young Japanese families
        I had befriended at the University of Illinois.
There were several young women
        in the group, and we discussed how their time
        as children in the US had been transformative.
They were totally opposed to the traditional
        role of Japanese women, and were busy

> reforming the Japanese work place
> to give equality to women.

What I was seeing over the years
> was the development of a uniquely
> Japanese culture entirely aware
> of its ancient roots, but which selectively
> adopted Western ways, when it suited.

Nothing was wrong with the vitality
> of this rejuvenated nation.

Our openhanded attitude towards our former enemies was a major factor in forming the international scene over the next half century after the war, and we succeeded in creating a "free world."

With the demise of the Soviet Union, it seemed we could claim a universal world leadership. Our place in future history books was assured.

V National Decline

And now, nearly a century after the war, we are a hegemon going through the stages of late maturity in step with every other historical example from Athens on. The specifics vary widely, and ours is particularly dramatic — having lost the precious balance between community spirit, individual freedom and equality that we used to think was uniquely ours, half of us are now convinced the postwar openhanded synthesis with which we led the world was totally wrong because we didn't claim the benefits of our domination for our direct pleasure in the ancient primitive way. The shocking suddenness of our turn is confirmed by the careless gutting of major federal institutions like the State Department under the Trump Administraton..

But the world doesn't wait for declining hegemons to sort themselves out, contenders just pile on to hasten the decline — witness the Russian grab for territory in the Ukraine and the Chinese grab for world dominance from a stumbling loser. In such a time the main problem is to avoid a childish tit-for-tat catastrophic war. It is important to realize collapsing cultures fill the annals of humanity, but along with the collapses are cases of enduring cultural vitality in the face of wrenching change.

All crisis periods share similarities, yet each has its own unique identity, and ours is especially dangerous because, in addition to the instability in our own country, it poses the new and universal threat of catastrophic climate change.

This period is not only one of decline, but also one of worldwide crises. First has been the covid pandemic, which isolated whole populations from normal contact in order to minimize infection. It lasted for years, and has killed five million people world-wide by the end of 2021. And it seems destined to become a permanent health problem.

The second crisis is more serious as it threatens climate upset. As a new kind of peril, climate change is outside the normal bounds of human history. It is caused by the great success and growth of our fossil-fueled technology over the past several centuries, coupled with a dramatic increase in population. In this century, we have reached critical levels of climate induced fires, *drought, and floods that impact economic and general living conditions world-wide. It is estimated that we may have only two decades to completely stop all use of fossil fuels, or face mortal perils to the entire biosphere.*

The extreme variety of these five periods is certainly disorienting, but at the end, we have played all our chips, and the people must generate clear eyed and wise leaders, or die.

For you, the next generation,
    not only must you live in this time of extreme hazard,
    you must shout out the rocks you see
    that can sink us all.
Though your voices seem drowned by thunderous rapids,
    and your waving arms dwarfed by the swells,
my beloveds,
    you must duck, row and pray.

And in the end, you need only
    unite in love.

VI Epilogue

Nature has known all along the potential
    we humans possess to remake
    Her original fiery cosmos
    into a new kind of All,
    guided by a love not yet fully imagined.

But hidden in the twisted chemical ladder
        that is our essence, is the possibility
        of retrogression when the path forward
        grows murky and uncertain
        or so fractious and conflict riven
        that a mistake is made,
        and the world of awareness we humans
        have come to typify is blown
        back into the deepest circle of hell.

Our particular danger lies
        in that ancient organ of our very self
        that made us the king of beasts.
        We haven't understood, though,
        that in that victory,
        the losers became our wards,
        and we now have a world to manage.

Only gods manage worlds,
        and only after winning our latest war
        — that with ourselves —
        will it be determined
        if humanity can achieve
        what has always been our destiny.

III

I

I am the feeling that feels
in the moment when my becoming becomes
and the present me tumbles
into what only the moment before
was the future.

It seems all too much like
some djinn playing ball,
but if so,
in the moment of being,
I put on the spin.

The Unfilled

Where have they gone —
those gods who filled
the ancient skies?

They fired
our empty souls
with passion —
but left us
in the dark.

A Valentine

I'm really old, my friend, and crotchety
about what I've failed at.

How can I say the world is your oyster,
when it isn't?
Rather, it is a new fight
for each generation,
and basically you are on your own.

But I love you with an abiding love,
and I'm ready to help you up
when you are convinced it is the end —
forgetting our up and down
history clear back to the trees.

Living Bonds

Standing naked in the midst of massed humanity,
I am in constant search for myself.

It isn't easy because there are as many selves
as there are separate communities in
the human landscape — one for my family,
another for my friends,
another for my town, and so on
through the enormous variety
of communities I belong to and serve.

In any given moment, when I have activated
a particular focus in that multiplicity,
I sense an enduring presence at my center,
which is the essential me, and it is that spirit
I find so elusive.

Those everchanging
communities I participate in
do not leave the central me unchanged —
so I am not the same self at day's end
as the one I began it with,
and that constant shaking and stirring
has consequences at depths
I didn't even know I had.

The central fact about who I am is
thus not to be found by digging
deeper in my center as if the truth
about me is like a seam of gold

to be discovered in the bowels
of a singular existence.
But rather, I am spread like butter
over a great landscape of multiplicity —
each community not a cold physical structure,
to be pulled apart and studied piece by piece,
but a kind of being all to itself,
held together by the sprinkle of love
contributed by each member.

In a human community
the bond I share is like a neuron
in my brain — a connection
with all the others who belong
to that community —

I am thus distributed over
a great piece of the human landscape,
not concentrated in one singular person
even though the physical nucleus
of my being is indeed so centered —
when it wears out and dies,
so do the living bond-neurons.

When I try to hold all this
in my rational mind at once,
it fails utterly, but instead
leaves me floating in feelings
of the vast ocean of living love
which is the essence of being alive.

Gimme that Old Time Religion

It's good 'nuff for you and me…
was a part of the lexicon teaching
the people how to love ever'body
and humans how to be a humanity.

We didn't think we could have made something
as divine as love even in bits and pieces,
so we made up stories about beings
much stronger and more god-like than we
who could, and who would pass it on to us.

Even though, hidden as we were,
and weak as we thought we were,
we turned the pottery wheel,
shaped the forms, and fired
the ovens ourselves,

and we called
it "Old Time Religion" or some other
catchy phrase to anchor it
in the spirit and hide the artist.

The ethereal visions growing
in our minds were holy, even though
they came from
our own lives and imaginings.

At first no one could believe
we had made such beauty,
and when the truth came out,
rejoicing filled the earth,
and lodged the creative will
of an empowered humanity
in its own living glow.

A Shapeless Thing

was thrust from the First World,
in the way Satan was thrown from heaven,
and established its domain not in a hell
but comfortably in our psyche
alongside love,

and no one knows what to do about it.

Altruism

is tit
without the tat,
oasis
without the desert,
grace
without reward

in all the All,
merely love.

Ancient and Cranky

I am like a bear in spring —
touchy and irritable,
my finish
is just around the corner,
and I have no idea
how to construct it.

I won't even tip my hat
to the archaic "Why,"
taunting us all from the first tick of time —
because it's evolution's top secret,
and no evolver knows diddly squat
about where he's bound.

So I work in ways I still can
on things I most care about,
and remember
some people may be watching.

So let them see me
still learning how to love.

Family

The ghostly presence
of Humanity in her flowered crown
floated over the Christmas party,
touching all of us with her
multipronged wand of love
which we proceeded to toss
back and forth to each other
like a baseball.

Glory was in the heavens that night.

Christmas

When I was very young,
and slept with my brothers
on the back porch of our tiny home,
Jesus' face was the last thing I saw
before sleep turned out my lights.

Soft words came from those precious lips,
in a private language all our own,
in a private world all our own.
It was my invitation to Be
in that world of privacy, from which
other worlds played out as if on TV screens,
but whose stories could be altered
on occasion if He and I worked together.
The love He dispensed so effortlessly
was the essence of our joint world,
and was a gift I could keep if I shared.

There came a time
when His image dimmed,
and like the spirit He was,
disappeared.
The world we had
made together remained
however,
and I realized He had been
what I now call imagination,
and the great TV screen morphed
into the vast external world
within which we are all embedded.

It was such a beautiful myth,
shared by so many,
that we set aside a day dedicated to it,
and call it Christmas.

His Legacy

When I looked over Mama's shoulder
with a growing awareness
of an immense world,
You appeared —
God on earth — lent from the joy
of my mother's religion
to fill that stone-cold realm
with a love that flowed
from your eyes to make a nest
that was the All for me.

As my world grew,
it could no longer fit the nest,
and You drifted off to fill
other imaginations.

You are gone,
but now I know a love
beyond all understanding
that can be turned like
the sun of a new Spring
on anyone, far or near,
as in memory I invoke once
more the life-giving mystery
of those eyes.

Mama

"Jesus, lover of my soul …"
The melody floated in the air
around my mother
as she did the chores of the house.
It saved her from the depths
that could have opened within her
the day she left Mississippi for love.

It was a double marriage,
one to Dad, and the second,
brought to life by the first,
rose on love from the deepest
corner of her soul, and cemented
her to a caring universe —
that new feeling thing in the world
that arose once there were caring
creatures to nurture it.

Me, Myself, and I

My deepest mystery
is also my greatest certainty
the "I" that dwells in my belly
is different from any other —

because to be
is to be me.

Love and Hate Together

Mankind is but a gaggle
of sticky we's,

where the highest grace
and acts of love,
and the basest deeds of cruelty
and joy of killing
cohabit the same person
in a hellish biology
even when planetary carnage threatens.

Nature, your human project
is broken and a failure,
and we have to remake ourselves,

but why have you made love
and hate brother and sister?

My Uncle Gabe

was a lawyer and community leader
in a small Mississippi town.
My mother adored him,
and was anxious for me to get to know him,
that I could more fully understand her.
So on one of my trips from El Paso
to college at that the University of Chicago,
I visited him.

"We Southerners love our 'Nigras,'"
he announced when we sat for lunch.
My newly acquired liberal views
were insulted and I flew to their defense.

Now I realize how naïve I was,
for I loved the Uncle Remus stories
I had read in the book
my grandmother had sent me as a child,
and had seen there the kind of love
that could develop between
an old slave and the young son
of his former master.

It was a story that sensitively explored
the roots of love between humans,
and it deeply affected me.
It was love in its most primitive
and basic form,
and it could exist alongside great wrong.

Now a living exemplar of that story
sat at table before me.
I was too naïve to recognize the rare chance
to explore a more human side
of the South many of us wanted to quash.

My Uncle Gabe died before
I could backtrack and "sit at his feet"
to learn how that love lived in him
alongside the wrong that still
existed even there and then.

This tragic drama playing out
between Uncle Gabe and me
sharply impacted my mother as well.

The love between her
and her brother was uncommonly deep,
and she clearly hoped I would look beyond
the flaws I might see to the goodness she saw
and, by extension, in the South
he lived in — which was also the South
of her own childhood and youth.

The brash fight I had with him
killed any hope I would,
by meeting her brother,
learn how she came to be the person
I so keenly loved and admired —
Sad.

Disarmed but not Disabled

Our hatred of the Evil Other
is the tool fixed in our psyche
from those times in the ancient jungle
when it was our secret weapon
in becoming the King of Beasts.

But with victory, we didn't disarm,
and have become, instead,
the Arch-Criminal of Beasts
for our many crimes against Nature.

If we cannot demilitarize ourselves,
certain death of all humanity awaits.

In the rush to save ourselves, however
we must take care not to conflate
all forms of assertiveness as one —
since the drive to create new beauty,
though a defanged form of aggression,
is the most blessed origin of all action.

For human change, like all change,
is ubiquitous, but when it flows
from a loving human heart,
the whole universe inches
forward in the glory of new life.

Betting on Mankind

What is he worth,
this current king of the jungle?

Nothing, if we continue
with business as usual,
the climate going to hell,
and species disappearing right and left.

But, should he wake up,
take in the impending train wreck,
and succeed in stopping it,
he is still only a stock
in an uncertain futures market.

But he has a once in eternity asset —
his ability to feel love and to forge Purpose,
unique in the known world.
It is an asset with a future value
which cannot be guessed.

Could this precious asset be the hope
of the entire unknown universe as well?

Humanity's Gamble

When Nature first invented evolution,
    all She knew was space, time, matter, and fire.
But when She invented life,
    it began to know itself
    and other selves through
    dimly transparent skins.
It was the borning of the subjective self,
    a whole new dimension of the universe.

Like a Cartesian graph,
    it is an axis with positive and negative
    extensions.
The positive half is love,
    which begins in the mother love
    manifest throughout the mammal world.

As they were still climbing down
    from the trees, they broadened it into
    a mutual caring for others of their tribe,
    till now when someone touches me gently
    and their eyes search mine for a response,
    I know I am loved.

That knowing and the love at its root
    is so precious, that to try to describe it
    takes us beyond words.
But still we pour them out,
    hoping the pile we produce
    will somehow glorify its existence.

Through it, our tribe ultimately became a nation
>   soaked in a rich culture that binds its people
>   into a rich community indicative
>   of our inherent sociality.

The negative axis of our subjectivity
>   is the competitive urge
>   to dominate a living space —
>   Darwin's criterion for self-survival,
>   which can become the deep hatred
>   of warfare.

With it we became the true King of Beasts,
>   to the amazement of everyone when
>   our brains proved more powerful
>   than fangs or size.

We won the reproductivity sweepstakes
>   and the only limit to our growth
>   was the carrying capacity of the planet —
>   now breached, to the accompaniment
>   of floods and burning forests,
>   with the lifeless state of planet Venus
>   just ahead.

The door to mankind's future is open
>   if we can find the key
>   and are able to share our laugh
>   with the other creatures.

The key is in our own myths
    where dwells a creator God
    whose very nature is love,
    who loves us unconditionally,
    being by being, and collectively as well.

This God is the aether bathing the subjective world
    lying beyond the earth and stars,
    but which in deep mystery, also guides
    the world of things through
    the power of purpose —
    the power of love.

We already know a whisper of this larger bonding
    when we fall in love with the world,
    feel at one with it, and melt inside ourselves
    in awe of it — this universe yearning
    for purpose.

Drunken Words

Those words chiseled
into the Jefferson Memorial,
"I have sworn on the altar of God
eternal hostility against every form
of tyranny over the mind of man,"
once meant what they said.

Now we lie like a cheap rug,
and can give words such a spin
that the most sacred become
giddy and frivolous.

But words like these are angels
from a Word Heaven
who never die.

The Next Comet

In the light of increasingly dire
climate warnings, has humanity
much chance of escaping
a mortal crisis?

The nature of the threat
and the parlous character
of human history says
"No, we're in for it, big time."

Being independent cusses, too many Americans
think they don't need to be told
about the climate —
they've read the weather all along,
and what can a couple of degrees of heat
do, anyway?

But this time, they are utterly and fatally wrong.
And their children and grandchildren
will mark their graves as enemies
of the human race, even if ignorant.

Heat waves will deny people their breath,
fires burn their forests and homes,
and monster hurricanes demolish
their seaside cities.

Refugees from heat blasted countries
will wander the earth
fleeing unlivable homelands
creating human Tsunamis
crushing peaceful frontiers.

We Americans
have pampered ourselves
back to a naive childhood
of fairy tale reality.

But people who devote their lives
to studying climate show
beyond scientific doubt there is little time left
to make fundamental changes in
the way we live.

For planetary astronomers
speculate Venus, a planet
hot enough to melt lead,
once had an atmosphere very like ours,
and succumbed to a runaway Greenhouse.

The next life-destroying comet
won't come from outer space —
but from our own swaggering vanity.

Love at First Sight

It was the birth
of our first child, a boy,
and I was looking through
a small window in the door
to the delivery room.

I could not stand still
as his head appeared slowly
from my wife's body.
And from ten feet in the air
where I dangled, I made a solemn vow
that this squalling chunk of humanity,
who in some strange way
made the three of us one,
would be the recipient
of all the love I could generate
through the fire hose
it seemed to gush from.

Was this the counterpart of
the famous mother love, that
flowed through her breast at feeding time?
I had no gushing milk — the fire hose I felt
was in my mind and heart.

He was only the first
the others were a wild mix
of prematurity and simply coming
ready-made through our front door.
Nevertheless, they were recipients

of the same love I learned how
to make the first time.

What is this love we parents have,
where does it come from,
and why is it so special?

Is it because the feelings
rising from a family dinner table
like the smoke from a candle
are the sinews of a family made stronger
yet more delicate by decades
of shared life, of triumphs and failures —
and something else unexpressible

how do you tell the song of a bird,
how do you name the joys of living a duet?

But I forget — biology speaks here
with its full force and clarity.
If it did not plant a feeling
stronger and deeper than death
in our psyches for the two we sowed,
how would the paired genes
from my mate and myself
survive a cruel world?

And for the other two,
would that cruel world itself survive

without sprinkles of grace
like those we blessed them with?

Plainly, this love comes from God.

Nature Amused

Nature outdid herself with us,
hinting maybe her successor,
but She kept an escape hatch,
now open and flaming.

But is it Funny?

On Being Great

Two happy faces said
I'm a Great Grand Dad to be.
I feel somehow different,
but don't know what I do.

When I look around
at the other people at lunch,
some of whom are also Great,
they seem relaxed, with sangfroid
to spare — maybe my new duties
will show up as needed.

So I throw out my chest,
and say "So am I —
just like you".

And now thank you, my dears
for conferring this new status
on me, tho the big change
is on you as you join
that great league of Parenthood.

May plentiful Blessings and Love
attend you all as your days roll
in that new beauty.

On Love

The birthday present that keeps on giving
is our mother's love,
which bloomed in the pain of birth,
and continues to morph
into the array of loves that tie us
to family and community.

Yet why do the pseudo joys
of personal triumph hold us in thrall,
when our victim's eye is forbidden to meet ours
in some misbegotten tribal pecking order?
Do we not know fear is no substitute
for respect and affection?

Where is the value
in a schizophrenic life
where half of us
is filled with the hatred still fueling
a bloody dominance struggle
for naked power in a world
hostile to gentler purpose,

when love is a gossamer bond
entwining us with the totality
of being in all its singular beauty
as we compound our uniqueness
within the community.

Old Love

They shine with an antique patina,
those couples who still find delight
in one another after young love
has faded.

Their children have miraculously grown up
just fine in spite of fearful nights,
and careers have become
merely retirements.

Each partner has tasted all they thought
the other had to give or withhold,
but no human goes round and round
like a clock.

For them, defeats come as often
as for us, but they have prepared
a soft landing in an easy lap,
and riposte is with two steadied minds
instead of the wild panic of one isolated.

Even tragedy is a shared loss,
rebuilt by a love thickened by decades
of practiced care.

And though their partnership is solid,
they are still two people, and know where
the layers of skin lie.

Everyone wonders if they still have sex,
and the answer is, some do, some can't.
But they all go to bed together at least
now and then, touching gently where time
has made a special spot.
And the thrill found there tells them
their love still lives.

This blessed few have found
the holy grail of the human condition,
and glow like great stars in a cold universe
that nevertheless hungers for new life.

Patriot

To be a working member of a true democracy
is to be a princeling on a white horse
in mankind's van on the way to its future
as builder and operator of a subjective loving
dimension within a cold and loveless universe.

We have unwittingly laid out this Way
in a beautiful myth about the son of God
appearing on earth to save us all
from a loveless and useless existence.

But other traits built into our character
have shown we are not yet ready,
and a time of heavy challenge is facing us
that will confirm our future, or kick us out
with the dinosaurs and dodoes.

To succeed, we will have to shed
a chunk of our overweening numbers,
and learn to be warders of other life
on a planet designed anew
for sustainability.

It will be a planet of love
and beauty and a delightful place
to live in, akin to the heaven
of our myths.

Schubert Piano Sonata in B-flat Major

I've been listening to you for years
and now leap ahead
to sit on keys in the deepest bass
waiting for you to do that isolated
deep rumble, a far thunder,
and then to race ahead a few bars
down-score, to draw you on.

It is the dark angel's interlude,
slipping in for all to hear,
an invitation to tea —
so we can get reacquainted
with the void we sprang from but forgot.

Surely there will be no compensation
from the shadowy gentleman
for your advertisement,

but please accept our thanks
for your music, which sits between
the void at either of its ends,
and points to humanity's gift
of an all-encompassing beauty,
lying in the very middle
of what before was only emptiness.

Stuck in Purgatory

Love and care
are matched in the human soul
by the hatred and violence we learned,
like Roman gladiators in an arena
where Nature and her gods cheered on
their champions, mimicking
those ancient barbarous times.

We were so good,
they invited us into the stands,
where we rival the vices of Nature, herself,
in blood lust and hunger for power.

Such experts in violence as we
need other creatures to practice on,
and since the only worthy candidates
are other humans, we struggle
against ourselves for tribal primacy,
with wholesale killing
of our own kind.

Shame be upon us, for this purgatory
our own genes have led us into.
The need, singular in its terrible urgency,
is for leaders with visions of a true humankind
who can liberate us from this broken biology.

How do the likes of us
breed such as them?

A Sunset

The blue-green planet
The green-blue earth
glows red
in the sunset.

We only burnt a measly bit of coal
to become the godly giants we are,
and look —
the whole world is set on fire!
We really didn't mean it —
Nobody meant to,
But somebody got mad,
And where on earth can we go now?

The beautiful blue-green planet
The beautiful green-blue heaven
glows red
in a self-made sunset.

The Living Land

In the way Native Americans revere the land
they are born to as a holy extension of themselves,
and though they have migrated continents,
each particular move is human sized,
and a deeply personal event.

The feeling for their land is enshrined
in chant and dance —
sung to the skies and nailed down as their own
in each step of the dance.

I felt this instinctive connection
for the land when the mountains
of Albuquerque hailed me
as I walked down the stairs
from my ABQ flight decades after
I had left home,
and returned for a brief visit,
not to my home town,
but to the Land of the Southwest.

In my mind, I had flung my arms wide
in reply to those welcoming and familiar
blue horizons, and gladly fell back
into their kin soaked world.

It was a living prancing land,
somehow my very own.

Last Laugh

When we stamp our feet,
the animals scatter in fear,
for we are the most violent
and powerful creatures on the planet.

We are also the most clueless
and cannot stop the lies
of our leaders or the widespread
repudiation of unpleasant realities.

Nature has the answer for such
foolish and benighted chutzpah,
and we won't like it
from where we will be.

When I Love my Friends

All Love derives from my mother
when she beckoned me to her arms
as a helpless baby.

It was the most profound
gift I received when I was born human,
and the warmth it generates in my soul
is a dimension of reality
measuring the depth of myself.

I don't every time go to the bottom
of my feeling self when I love someone,
but the whole depth always beckons,
and when fully searched leads me
into that mystical world we experienced in our creation
of the spirit worlds set out in our bibles —
and even before that, as we drank the milk
of life from our mother's breast.

So love is life at its far limit,
experienced as a feeling that
we have tried for eons to set to words,
but always find ourselves, instead searching
for words beyond words.
just as in this poem, I reach for it,
but not nearly far enough

to bring it home.

The Two Ways

From the beginning of life,
there have been two Ways —
the first, be generous and altruistic with
people within your family or your tribe,
and, second., be deadly killers or exploiters
of everyone and everything without.

These are the rules of Darwinian evolution,
and humans still obey its laws in maturity,
like an overgrown teenager,
who cannot put away his childish things.

But these are tools of the kill,
not things of play.

Whose Country

The Times are "interesting"
in that famous way,
and our national community
seems to be so delicately
balanced the most benign
comment would topple it.

Each side is convinced
the other will be the end
of the country as they know it.
Both are right:

One side remembers the past
of their fathers and grandfathers,
and knows the future of the other side
will be unrecognizable because
ethnic minorities will become
ethnic majorities and their old country
will disappear.
They are right.

The other side remembers
their fathers and grandfathers
knew their country was imperfect,
and must change to a Future
only the future will fully understand.
They are also right.

The Conservers are ready to fight,
the Reformers will defend the
Idea of America they grew up with.
Is conflict and violence the only way?

Digital Futures

Artificially intelligent computers
will soon be able to learn
about the world faster and better
than humans do.

What will their relation to us be?
Will they be malleable servants?
or ...
Will they be our masters?

Surely both of us
would be best served
in collaboration, like
the shepherd and his dog.

But time is short, and questions abound.
Would they know consciousness?
And would they know love,
or only the dry coldness of their logic?

Challenge

It's awful out there —
wars, pandemics, failing politics,
fires and hurricanes from climate change,
even mass species extinction.
How can we live through all that?

Well, maybe we won't,

but if we do, it will be
like those other times,
when something deep inside shouts
"Yes,"
and, all together, we will
stand up, duck our heads,
and fight like hell.

It is deeply buried
till we need it,
and then as the skies open,
we become giants with god's
shields and spears and nothing
seems impossible.

Awe and Admiration

As life discovered how an external skin
could shield its delicate and complex
processes from the turbulent world,
the single cell world took off,
and if a single cell could live,
multiple cells could too,
and biology exploded.

It was a momentous point
in the evolution of the universe —
self-awareness was paired with life,
and in a cold world of physics,
a whole new dimension was added.

In the known world, we humans
may be at the apex of that development,
and a compelling question is
"What's next?"

Given the level of turmoil behind us,
it is likely to be furious.

Telepathy, and a magnified consciousness
come to mind,
but it is a more likely to be beyond
our relatively feeble imagination to contemplate.

Only awe and admiration are relevant.

Why Not

"Why Not"
must come from the heart
for its potency to be real.

For there are horrid times ahead,
for the younger people
I know and love, and also
for the others yet unknown to me.

I, my peers and forebears,
failing in our duty,
have bequeathed to our posterity
a Mankind in trouble.

The menacing clouds we see
prove those who will live after me
must suffer the unprecedented storm
gathering there.

The tempest stirs in me already
with imagined furor,
and my peace is upended
by my own emotional preparation
for their trials.

How can I pass on to them
who will live that horror
some of my own strength,
so they will feel the long ties
that bind them to eons
of human growth and wisdom —
now deposited in their sinews,
ready to unite all humans
in the struggle.

They must feel they can and will
meet and overcome the dark time,
thus preparing humanity to claim
its immense destiny as the soul
of an emerging universe.

May this struggle be but the birthing
pains of that great beauty.

Our Duty

Some say the earth now belongs to us,
but look what we have done with it:

A sixth extinction of all other life.
Climate run-away.
A population getting too large to feed,
and so fractious we are nearly impossible to lead . . .

We are made with all-natural ingredients,
except for our conscious mind.
And that is so new we are like a test model rocket —
needing constant supervision.

But, with it,
we are Nature's potential masterpiece.
We have created at its center a world of feels,
which we have used to create a quality of love
never before experienced in a cold unknowing universe.

If Nature held a God,
we have dreamt its traits,
and know full well our destiny
as a key entity in an unfeeling universe.

This is the great challenge to us:
Realize our potential and destroy the devils
within us who chain us to the hell
we now occupy.

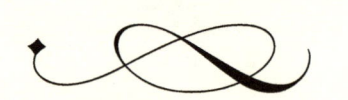